GAIETY THEATRE AYR – Tel.: AYR (0292) 64939

WEEK COMMENCING MONDAY, 25th OCTOBER, 1976

NIGHTLY at 6.25 and 8.40 p.m.

DUGGIE CHAPMAN
present

The Broons & Oor Wullie – Mair Music Please!

First published 2013 by DC Thomson Annuals Ltd.
Courier Buildings, 2 Albert Square, Dundee DD1 9QJ
Scotland, UK

The Broons and *Oor Wullie* are Copyright © 2013 and Registered ® 2013
D.C. Thomson & Co. Ltd.
www.dcthomson.co.uk

The publishers gratefully acknowledge the help and assistance of Colin Calder and Bob Bain, in providing posters, programmes and other decorative material reproduced in this book, including images first published by Lawrence Wright Music Co. Ltd.; Howard Wyndham Ltd.; Chappell & Co. Ltd.; James S Kerr; Pete Davis; The Clover Music Co. Ltd.; Mozart Allan; Noel Gay Music Co. Ltd.

Performances and posters relate specifically to The Gaiety Theatre, Ayr; The Glasgow Empire; The Metropole, Glasgow; The King's Theatre, Edinburgh; The Alhambra, Glasgow; The Palace Theatre, Dundee; The Pavilion Theatre, Glasgow; The King's Theatre, Glasgow. Notable presenters for performances spotlighted include: Stewart Cruikshank, Fraser Neal and Leslie A. Macdonnell.

The publishers also thank The Royal Edinburgh Military Tattoo Office for their help and co-operation, and The Glebe Street Barber (Comb-Over Specialist), Glebe Street, Auchentogle, for kind permission to reproduce their award-winning promotional comb.

Design and layout by Hugo Breingan
Cover Artwork: Ken Harrison

ISBN: 978-1-84535-511-1

Printed and bound in China

Tickets : £1.00   75p   45p

...UCTION RATES FOR CHILDREN AND PENSIONERS EACH PERFORMANCE EXCEPT SATURDAY

PRINTED BY A. TAYLOR & SONS LTD., WOMBWELL, BARNSLEY, SOUTH YORKSHIRE.

MOSS'
Empire
THEATRE GLASGOW

Telephone: Douglas 6434-5-6
Chairman & Joint Managing Director: PRINCE LITTLER
Joint Managing Director: LESLIE A. MACDONNELL
Proprietors: MOSS' EMPIRES LTD.
Manager: FRANK MATHIE

6-25 — Monday, MARCH 2nd — 8-40

★ "WHITE HEATHER" GROUP ★

SONGS OF SCOTLAND

Radio & T.V. Favourite

ROBERT WILSON · JOE GORDON FOLK FOUR · ANDY STEWART

Bothy Balladiers

DESMOND CARROLL ★ ANGUS FITCHETT ★ KISTER KRONIES

TERRY O'DUFFY **SYDNEY DEVINE** TOMMY LOMAN

GORDON MacKENZIE BILLY CROCHET AND JEANNIE Mad Musicians WILL STARR

Singing Star of Glen Alsia

12 WHITE HEATHER GIRLS 12

ACE ACCORDIONIST

THE WHITE HEATHER **CORNKISTERS**

RICHARD WHEWELL (BOLTON) LTD.

Mair Music Please

IN 'Mair Music Please' The Broons and Oor Wullie celebrate all manner of music.

From the earliest days of the strips appearing in The Sunday Post, music has never been far away and The Broons and Oor Wullie have become as famous as many of the legends and stories which weave the fabric of Scotland's Traditional Music.

Scotland's music reflects and records the daily lives and loves of the Scot whether highlander or lowlander, borderer or islander, over hundreds of years – songs and melodies handed down over generations preserved by our bards and storytellers, monks and scholars, minstrels and travelling folk.

Scotland's music continues to be celebrated by musicians with harps, pipes, flutes, fiddles, accordions, guitars, drums and whatever other instruments that come to hand, with singers and dancers up and down the land and wherever Scots are to be found in the world.

The Broons family and Oor Wullie and his pals play their part – some with greater ability than others it must be said, but if enthusiasm and passion are musical barometers, then a great atmosphere is always guaranteed.

Scotland's songs and ballads are of popular heroes – how they lived, loved and died– there are songs of rebellion – of land-hungry Scots and land-owners – there are songs of war – songs of country and city folk – songs of sadness – songs of joy – of Scotland's pride – of delight in the beauty of hills and glens lochs and rivers. Since 1936 The Broons & Oor Wullie scriptwriters and illustrators over the years have entertained us with many musical interpretations and celebrations where music and song dominates the occasion – be it a Burns Supper, a weddin' or a dance at The Boolin' Club.

These celebrations are of a courageous, passionate and romantic music culture – from folk music that represents the combined musical taste of its singers and hearers (as old as time itself) and that comes alive at the hands of each musician and singer, to classical styles originally influenced by the church and state – and it doesn't stop there!

Our favourite family is always ready to embrace different forms of music; over the years jazz, pop, skiffle – musicals and even opera.

GLEBE STREET RECORDS

Viva-tonal Recording

AULD LANG SYNE
GLASGOW PHOENIX CHOIR

35-75-B

Ae Fond Kiss

Robert Burns

Ae fond kiss, and then we sev - er! Ae fare - weel. then for ev - er! Deep in heart - wrung tears I'll pledge thee,

The Glebe Street Barber
COMB-OVER SPECIALIST

Ae fond kiss, and then we sever!
Ae fareweel, alas! For ever!
Deep in heart-wrung tears I'll pledge thee,
Warring sighs and groans I'll wage thee.

The Broons are indeed a multi-talented family. Remember for example, The Broons family wi' Paw Broon conductin' – *The Brahms Lullaby* like ye never heard it afore. Maggie on Piano, Horace on violin, Daphne an the Bairn on Percussion, The Twins on paper comb an' moothie, Joe on accordion, Hen on bugle and ukulele, Granpaw on the pipes an' Maw on the chair.

And Oor Wullie – a musical lad – of that there is no doubt!

Whether it is hummin' on a comb wi' a bit greaseproof paper or conjuring a tune from a moothie or drumming on his bucket, he is always ready to take centre stage and continue the traditions and explore new musical territory.

And there's nae excuse for you folk not to join in – there's a comb kazoo included with this book so gather a few freins – gather round that old piano, roll up the carpet and get going with a céilidh and a sing-song!

THE BROONS

The Sunday Post - 12th February 1939

See "Duchess" Daphne raise a smile —
When she comes riding home in style!

The Sunday Post - 16th March 1941

The Sunday Post - 28th December 1941

Upstairs, downstairs, round the town —
Piano-shifting gets Paw down.

The Sunday Post - 4th May 1947

On this page you'll understand—
How the Bairn beats the band.

The Sunday Post - 5th April 1942

THE BROONS

The Sunday Post - 1st January 1939

THE BROONS

The Sunday Post - 22nd March 1942

Here the Bairn you can see—
Sailing the good ship "Fiddle-de-dee".

The Sunday Post - 10th August 1941

Gran'paw's dose of a "one-man band"
Wasna the cure the doctor planned.

The Sunday Post - 4th April 1943

The Sunday Post - 28th December 1947

THE BROONS

The Sunday Post - 19th December 1948

The Sunday Post - 6th June 1948

The Sunday Post - 13th January 1952

ARE YE DANCIN'?

WHAT do William Wallace, Robert the Bruce, Angus Og, Bonnie Prince Charlie, Sir Walter Scott, Sir Harry Lauder and Sean Connery all have in common – besides being Scottish? They all met their wives by saying: 'Are ye dancin'?'

It's the question that launched a million relationships. If you were lucky you heard: 'Are ye askin'?'. If you were unlucky it was: 'Naw it's just the way am standin'' … or much worse.

It's all changed now, of course – and it was always changing. People have been dancing at ceilidhs since the beginning of time and no one has ever felt the need to stop.

Within 50 years of the first public dance halls opening, around the 1870s, most people did one of two things with their spare time: they went to the pictures or they went to the dancin'.

A technological advance in the 1920s spurred the dancin' on: the charabanc, the forerunner to the modern bus. A charabanc could take you door-to-door from one village hall to another

■ The house band at Burntisland Palais, 1948
Pictures: Burntisland Heritage Trust

BURNTISLAND PALAIS DE DANSE
ROBERT HUTTON, Proprietor and Manager
"Where youth and pleasure meet
To chase the glowing hours with flying feet."
WEDNESDAY - POPULAR NIGHT
8 to 11. Ladies 9d.: Gents 1/-:
SATURDAY - CARNIVAL NIGHT
8 to 11. Ladies 1/-: Gents 1/6.
SPECIAL DANCES
arranged during Holidays
THE MOST POPULAR PALAIS WITH THE PERFECT FLOOR
MANSE LANE
BURNTISLAND

and concert parties could travel. A few weeks later their new friends returned the favour.

When World War II began in 1939 all public dance halls were closed. It didn't seem right to be having fun while there was a war on. A few weeks later, though, the powers-that-be realised that fun was exactly what people needed – and the dancin' began again.

The war brought another phenomenon to Scotland: Americans. Scottish women found GI dance partners and some even

married them. It was the climax of the big band era. By the post-war era, jazz, the 'noise' your parents hated, was completely mainstream. The dancin' had become the centre of most people's social lives.

As Scotland arrived in the 1950s change was in the air. Its ears were open to new music, including the rock'n'roll which was beginning to make an impression via Elvis and Bill Haley, among others. America brought us new dance steps: this was the jive era..

Lonnie Donegan had started a

■ A 1920s charabanc – exposed and top heavy.
Picture: Portnellan Highland Lodges

SHONA WALLACE: There were about fifteen of us in our concert party and at least once every six weeks it was our turn to go out and perform somewhere else.
The charabanc bus was often a cold thing to be in. There was a canvas roof which came over if it rained, but it didn't keep any heat in. So sometimes you'd be frozen to the bone. One night it toppled over on the road out to Spean Bridge.

CHERRY GRANT was a well-known character in Dunfermline's Kinema Ballroom in the 1940s. She taught dancing but is most remembered for her role as hostess. If you misbehaved you had to answer to her – although most people didn't dare.

Picture: Brian Nobile Archive

music craze, based on American folk, that had made guitar sales soar: skiffle. Elsewhere in the UK, a young man by the name of Lennon put together a skiffle group called the Quarrymen. Who was listening to this new music? That new invention: the teenager. Spurred on by the American influence, teenagers were inventing their own scene. In the late 50s it was the aim to style your hair in a quiff, slip on

a bootlace tie: the Teddy Boy was born.

■ *Extract from* **Are Ye Dancin'?** *by Eddie Tobin and Martin Kielty, published by Waverley Books 2010.*

■ Above: a typical night at the JM Ballroom in Dundee in the 1950s.
■ Clothes were of prime importance to the Teddy Boys.
Picture: Stewart Campbell

ROY KITLEY: When I was 15 I set up the Pythons Skiffle Group. We cribbed the name from the Vipers, one of the big groups of the time. We were kept really busy with cinema gigs, church socials, parties and dances. It really did happen overnight and suddenly there were thousands of groups, sometimes several in one street, and the rivalry was pretty fierce.

■ The Pythons Skiffle Group.
Picture: Roy Kitley

Maw and Daph and Maggie too—
Think Gran'paw should be in the zoo!

The Sunday Post - 20th April 1952

The Sunday Post - 31st May 1953

The Sunday Post - 11th January 1953

Hen plays a tune, and sweet notes come –
Rising out o' the cottage lum!

The Sunday Post - 14th November 1954

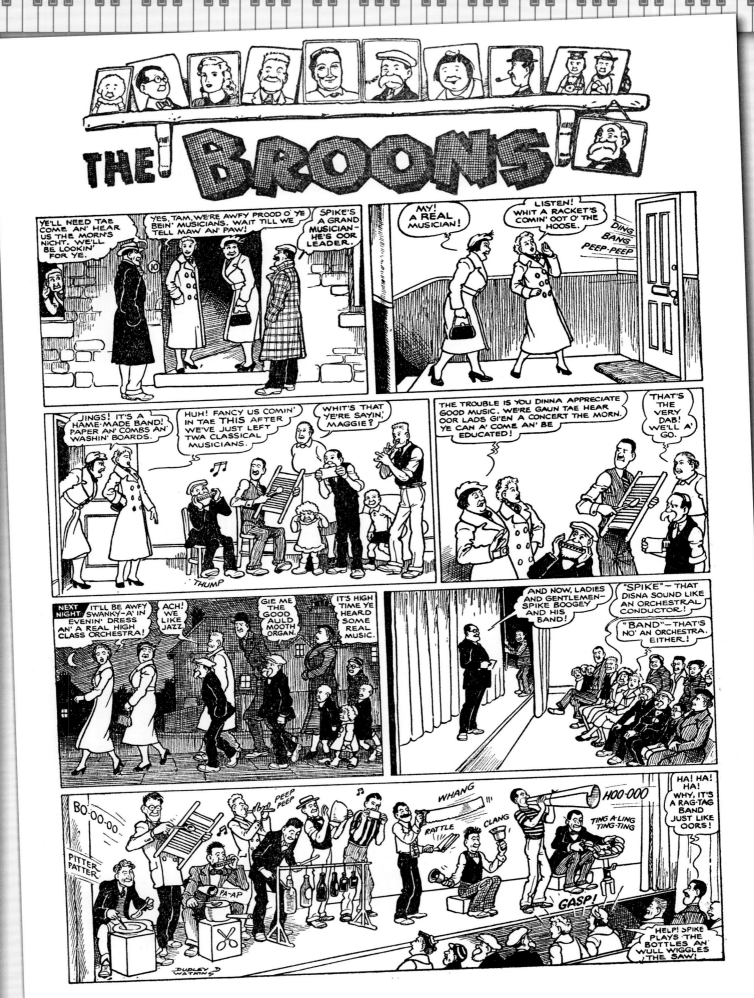

The Sunday Post - 30th January 1955

The Broon folks make an awfy racket—
But their new neighbours sure can tak' it!

The Sunday Post - 7th September 1958

The Sunday Post - 12th May 1957

The Bairn thinks these Country Dancers—
are maybe just a lot o' chancers!

The Sunday Post - 2nd April 1961

The Sunday Post - 30th January 1964

The Sunday Post - 8th October 1967

When it comes to making noise —
You must admit, MEN will be boys

The Sunday Post - 27th September 1974

The Sunday Post - 20th September 1964

The family's noisy, that's a fact—
So poor Paw reads the QUIET act!

The Sunday Post - 14th December 1975

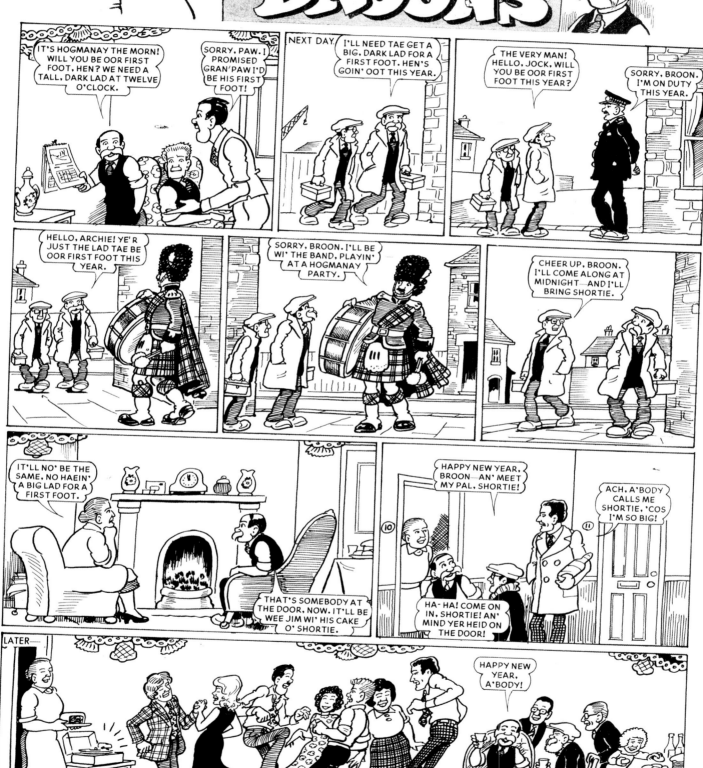

The Sunday Post - 30th December 1979

ARE YE ASKIN'?

In Scotland's music scene there'd been rock'n'roll, then skiffle, followed by jive dancing. In 1960 Chubby Checker tore a big hole through the middle of dancing culture when he gave us 'The Twist'. It introduced a new style: 'dancing apart to the beat'.

Suddenly it was 'no touching' except for the slow dances – and it was preferred. It was a lot easier to twist than it was to jive or follow the steps of a strict-tempo dance. If you look at it one way, it gave expression back to the masses. If you look at it another, it spoiled a fine tradition. The future was in beat music, it

> **BILL GRACIE:** Things happened quite slowly but I think for the public the big changes were: you didn't have to buy a book full of dance steps, you didn't have to wear your Sunday best and you could just jump about like a demented dervish to pull the birds.

seemed, and the evidence was provided by the rise of the beat clubs which slowly saw the ballrooms' grip on the scene fall away.

Perhaps the old world of ballroom dancing could have kept jiving and rock'n'roll at bay – but the beat boom was to be so big it even took over the United States, something everyone in the British entertainment industry dreamed of.

It wasn't a wipe-out right away – as long as people still wanted the more formal style of dancing, ballrooms were there to provide it. Some ballrooms banned jiving and teenagers – they tried to ban beat groups too. But many musicians embraced the new style as another turn of the wheel of life.

The paying public had never been so spoiled for choice – the beat groups were getting their fair share of the game and, for a time, the older bands were still being given their place.

Travel was easier – with the Forth Road bridge and other travel improvements – so dancers could travel further afield. But by the

■ The Beatles in their early days at a small Scottish club.
Picture: Stewart Campbell.

> **FRANCES LYTTLE:** I was at the Locarno one Saturday night with my friend Ethel – seven and six was the entry fee for the night. We thought the talent was not so good and we decided to head off, but, just then, a boy asked Ethel to dance. She took one look at him and refused, to which he quickly replied: 'What do you want for seven and six ... Rock Hudson?'

late sixties music was evolving again– Pink Floyd, Cream and Jimi Hendrix – clever music you listen to rather than dance to. The bands forgot about dressing up and putting on a show, and playing for dancing to.

The 1970s heralded the rock movement and also the discos. DJ's became celebrities.

The years between the 1940s and the early 1970s saw regular changes to the dance hall scene. Many types of music, types of dance and types of venues flourished then died as progress kept moving forward. But by the mid-70s sound systems started sounding much better. The

■ The Alex Harvey Soul Band rehearsing.
Picture: James Grimes

result was the death of bands in clubs, because you couldn't make a band sound the way new records did.

The 1980s nightclubs were still about dancin' and winchin' but ballroom disappeared. Dunfermline's Kinema Ballroom became Night Magic. Light shows and lasers and neon lights became the entertainment. And the 1990s gave us Acid House and high-energy dance music, that would have been totally alien to the Kinema's clientele in the 40s.

Now in the 2000s ballroom is back. *Strictly Come Dancing* has awoken an interest in paired dancing once again. The dance goes on, as it's been going for hundreds of years. You can be sure of one thing: underneath the glitz and glamour, the clothes, and the tunes will be that age-old question that starts everything off everywhere: 'Are ye dancin'?'

■ *Extract from* **Are Ye Dancin'?** *by Eddie Tobin and Martin Kielty, published by Waverley Books 2010*

THE ELGIN FOLK MUSIC CLUB
Presents
The "Love Me Do" Boys
THE BEATLES
plus
The Alex. Sutherland Sextet
in
THE TWO RED SHOES
on
THURSDAY, 3rd JANUARY
9 p.m. - 1 a.m.   Admission 6/-.
Buses return to Buckie, Forres, Coast, Lossiemouth, etc.

THERE WERE four of them but they weren't fab just yet. In January 1963, the Beatles failed to arrive for their show in Keith so the first one they played was at the Two Red Shoes in Elgin. The house band, the Alex Sutherland Sextet, were being relied on to lift the audience numbers. Just 80 people were there.

■ Glasgow's Picasso Club: to play there and not be booed off you had to be okay.

EXTRACT FROM RULES

1. No intoxicating liquor will be brought into or consumed in the Club.
2. Members only allowed one guest per evening.
3. The management reserves the right to refuse admission.
4. Membership card must be produced on request.
5. Members will be responsible for their guests.

NAME
ADDRE
DATE
SIGNATU

CLUB PICASSO
200 BUCHANAN STREET
GLASGOW, C.1

MEMBERSHIP CARD

■ Da Vinci's nightclub in Dundee in the 1980s. Picture: Gordon Girvan

Jings, what a shock—
Gran'paw likes "rock"!

The Sunday Post - 8th June 1980

The Sunday Post - 14th June 1981

This you must see—
A duet for THREE!

The Sunday Post - 5th August 1981

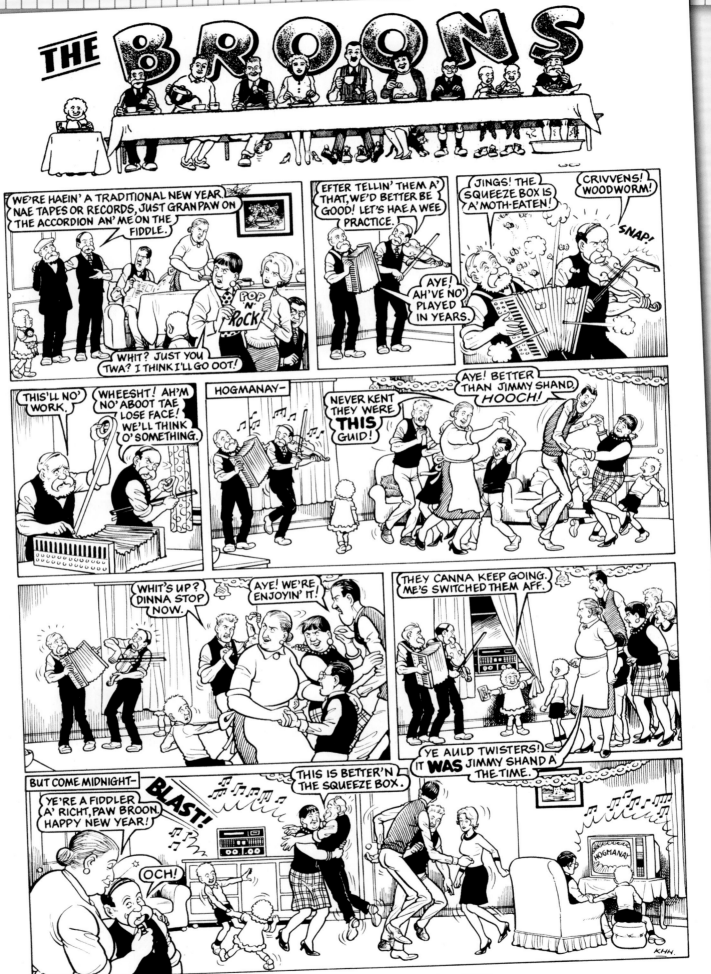

The Sunday Post - 30th December 1990

Granpaw in a boxing match?
Aye, but listen—there's a catch!

The Sunday Post - 28th January 1990

The Sunday Post - 3rd March 1991

The Sunday Post - 22nd October 1995

The Sunday Post - 3rd January 1993

Hen canna wait tae meet his date!
She's a cracker! Ah, but wait . . .

The Sunday Post - 28th June 1992

Nae record player, harp or spoons—
Can hold a candle tae these loons!

The Sunday Post - 5th January 1992

The Sunday Post - 19th February 1995

The Sunday Post - 2nd January 1994

At Number Ten on Hogmanay—
—it's music an' dancin' all the way?

The Sunday Post - 31st December 1995

COUNTRY DANCING

Scottish Country Dance is a style of social dance which is a unique blend of music and dancing, involving groups of couples of dancers following highly disciplined, intricately choreographed steps and arm and hand movements.

(Not to be confused with Scottish Highland dance which is a solo dance, a performance which is the subject of keen competition at highland gatherings and games across the world.)

Today the name Country Dance generally refers to all of the social dances which have become popular and are danced across the world.

In ancient times dancing formed part of a religious ceremony, as it still does in some religions in the world.

It was also undoubtedly a means of poetic expression.

Dancing took on quite a stately air and became part of the great Court ceremonies of Louis XIV of France, who did much to popularise dance. Dance evolved, became a pleasure, and quite frolicsome variations became the talk of the day.

When the Waltz was first introduced early in the nineteenth century, it was seen as being quite indecent!

When we take to the floor we take part in an international experience. We thank Poland for The Polka and the Mazurka – Germany for the Schottische and Galop and the Waltz and look across the Atlantic for Jazz and the Boston, but Scotland and Ireland gave us the Reel and Jig respectively.

But there are rules and principles based on the laws of balance and grace which need to be followed unless of course you are a guest at Auchentogle's Co-operative Ha' or The Auchentogle's Young Farmers' Cèilidh or a similar social gathering, where the rules can be relaxed and often interpreted differently, particulary when The Broons are present.

The Reel is a national dance of Scotland, but is similar to the Kreol of Denmark, but of course the Scots declare that it was they who introduced the dance into Scandinavia.

It usually consists of a number of springing steps and often quite

I BET I'D LOOK BRAW IN A KILT!

HO! HO! THERE'S WULLIE WISHIN' HE WIS GOIN' IN FOR THE DANCIN' TAE!

exaggerated gesticulation, and the music is in 4-4 or 6-4 time. There is a slow variety called the Strathspey, and a faster version danced in Ireland.

The term 'country dance' doesn't take its name from any rustic origin. The term is a corruption of the French *centre*, meaning opposite, as in most country dances the partners stand opposite one another in long lines, the ladies in one line the gentlemen in the other.

The origins of dancing in Scotland are fairly obscure with no specific mention in early documentation until the 16th century.

There is mention of the Hebridean singing of a *port-a-bail* (a mouth tune) in the 12th century and it is thought that this would be accompanied by dancing but generally in Scotland, just as in Europe, it was not until the 17th century that dancing became popular.

Musical instruments were the key. First came the viol, then the fiddle and it was that instrument which played a significant part in allowing dancing to emerge as the new vogue for social interaction.

Mary Queen of Scots had a reputation of being an excellent dancer and that apparently added to her charming the French court. With one European court frequently influencing the other it meant that new ideas of style and content were adopted and it is likely that Mary helped introduce it on her return to Scotland.

In the Elizabethan court of England rustic figure dances called 'country dances' were popular and these were mostly set to Celtic tunes. By the late 16th century new European ideas changed many aspects of Scottish society including the music of the day which changed from the harp to the pipes. It is at this time that the word reel first appears and in the following century ports, possibly the forerunner of slow Strathspeys are also recorded.

Dancing was part of Edinburgh life for the aristocracy by the early 1700s.

By the 1740s Edinburgh was showing signs of a changing modern style of life with all the trappings of commerce and polite culture. Taverns sponsored regular concerts by amateur musicians and the city became the music capital of Scotland and the dances continued borrowing from reels and jigs and strathspeys and the range of what we know as Scottish Country Dances became established.

The Royal Scottish Country Dance Society (RSCDS) is the organisation dedicated to upholding and promoting Scottish country dance in Scotland and across the world.

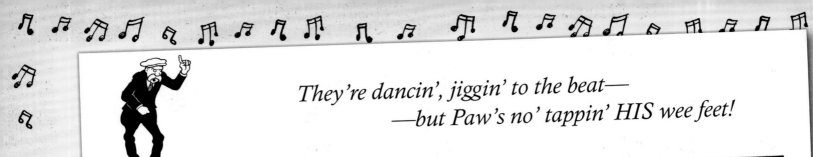

They're dancin', jiggin' to the beat—
—but Paw's no' tappin' HIS wee feet!

The Sunday Post - 18th September 1994

The Sunday Post - 30th June 1996

The Sunday Post - 2nd June 1996

There's an ootside change—
—there'll no' be a dance!

The Sunday Post - 31st March 1996

An evenin' at the concert hall,
Means culture calls for one an' all.

But somebody'll need a hand,
When left abandoned by his band.

Scotland's Musical Theatre

Scotland's theatres have been home to drama, opera, comedy and tragedy and musical theatre. These theatrical stage performances combining song and dance became popularly known as 'musicals'.

Musical theatre began to grow in the 19th century with Gilbert & Sullivan's comic operas such as *The Mikado*, *HMS Pinafore* and *The Pirates Of Penzance* capturing the imagination of audiences, to be followed later by the American influence of musicals by Jerome Kern, Rodgers and Hart, Cole Porter and George Gershwin.

These led to an era which saw shows like *Oklahoma*, *Show Boat* and *West Side Story* which set the stage for a continuing fascination with the musical and the world has since been entertained with *Hair*, *Chorus Line*, *Phantom Of The Opera* and so many others.

The theatres themselves saw melodrama, pantomime and variety with music hall artistes touring across numerous venues in Scotland, many of them becoming household names – such as Marie Lloyd, Sarah Bernhardt, Will Fyffe and of course Harry Lauder, an international Scottish entertainer hailed by Sir Winston Churchill as "Scotland's greatest ever ambassador!" Sir Harry wrote many of his own songs, *Roamin' in the Gloamin'*, *I Love a Lassie*, *A Wee Deoch-an-Doris*, and *Keep Right on to the End of the Road*.

The Pavilion Theatre in Glasgow began to host pantomimes in the 1930s with top name stars of the Scottish variety scene, such as Harry Gordon and Dave Willis and hosted most of the well-known music hall stars over the years, and in the 1930s became known for its pantomime tradition with Harry Gordon and Dave Willis, followed later by Jack Anthony and the tradition continued with names such as Lex McLean and Jack Milroy.

Lulu, Lena Zavaroni, Sheena Easton, Barbara Dickson, Billy Connolly, Hector Nicol and Andy Cameron are but a few of the stars who ensured packed houses at The Pavilion.

The Alhambra Theatre Glasgow opened in 1910 with a 2,800 seating capacity, a revolving stage, and

THE METROPOLE THEATRE

PROUDLY PRESENTS

Scotland's Comedy Queen

GRACE CLARK

AND HER MAN

COLIN MURRAY

In Moments of Laughter!

They are the Greatest!

THE ONLY THEATRE IN GLASGOW

Where the Fabulous

ALEXANDER BROS.

Can be Seen

SEE & HEAR THEM
AT THE METROPOLE

STARS OF TELEVISION,
RADIO & PYE RECORDS

RIKKI FULTON AND JACK MILROY
as Francie and Josie in
Babes in the Wood
KINGS EDINBURGH

EMPIRE 6.25 FOR ONE WEEK ONLY MONDAY, 26th FEB. 8.40
GLASGOW—300gdns 4424/5/6
GLEN MUSIC presents A STAR STUDDED VARIETY BILL
A TOAST TO THE TARTAN
The Golden Voice of The Highlands and Dance Recording Star
CALUM KENNEDY
Special Guest Stars
CHIC MURRAY & MAIDIE   JOE GORDON FOLK FOUR
BACK AGAIN!
From TV's "Spot The Tune"   From Las Vegas
Your Favourite Entertainer
BILLY RAYMOND
McANDREWS & MILLS   WILL STARR   HOLLANDER & HART
Dance Team
ANNE GILLIES   ALEX DONN AND NICK NICHOLS
Radio and TV Star   Musical Nonsense
Admission   5/- 4/- 3/- and 2/6

ANN FIELDS
COLIN STUART
RAE GORDON
BILLY LITTLE
VI DAY
DANNY REGAN
GEO. REX
10 MOXON MAIDS

COLIN STUART   ANN FIELDS

LES BALADINS
FROM THE LIDO, PARIS

Booking Form

To The Manager,
THE METROPOLE THEATRE, St. George's Cross, Glasgow, C.3.

Dear Sir,
    Please book the following seats for my party:—

STALLS.............................6.25 | 8.30 | Matinee   Date.............

CIRCLE.............................6.25 | 8.30 | Matinee   Date.............
                    (Please delete performance not required)

Matinees every Saturday as from 2nd December at 2.15 p.m.
Holiday Matinees 25th December, 1st, 2nd, 3rd & 6th January, 1968.

PRICES OF ADMISSION:—
Monday to Thursday, 1st House Friday and Saturday Matinees   STALLS, 7/6 CIRCLE, 6/6
2nd House Fridays, Saturdays and Holidays   STALLS, 8/6 CIRCLE, 7/6
All Performances 25th December—6th January (Inclusive) at Holiday Prices

Name...

Address.....................................
....

PLEASE BOOK EARLY—BOOKING OFFICE Telephone—DOUglas 9191-9192 (2 Lines)
PLEASE DETACH AND POST TO MANAGER

Jimmy Logan's
METROPOLE
Glasgow

1967 - Winter Show - 1968   6.25 - Twice Nightly - 8.30
PRODUCED BY DANNY REGAN & JIMMY LOGAN

THE FABULOUS
ALEXANDER BROTHERS
** AND **
BILLY RUSK
** IN **
'SCOTLAND THE BRAVE'

GRAND GALA PERFORMANCE THURSDAY, 23rd NOVEMBER AT 7.30 P.M.

---

specialised in variety. The stage was rebuilt in 1961 to be the Starlight Room for the Five Past Eight shows which featured such entertainers as Rikki Fulton, Jimmy Logan, Stanley Baxter, Kenneth McKellar, Max Bygraves and Frankie Vaughan who became stars of the new television era.

The Glasgow Empire was originally the Gaiety Theatre which opened its curtains for the first time in 1874 becoming a music hall within ten years. In 1896 it was replaced by the Empire Palace which opened the following year. In 1930 it was reconstructed and extended to the corner of Renfield Street, seating 2,100 in comfort and topping the bill were Jack Payne and the BBC Dance Band.

The last performance at the Empire was on Sunday 31st March 1963 by an all-star cast who came to say goodbye to this famous variety theatre which had hosted many stars over the years including many from the USA: Rosemary Clooney, Lena Horne, Betty Hutton, Judy Garland, Kitty Kallen, Ella Fitzgerald, Eartha Kitt, Frankie Laine, Johnnie Ray, Hoagy Carmichael, Jerry Colonna, Mel Tormé, Don Cornell and Frank Sinatra.

Amongst the comedians who took the stage: Jack Benny, Abbott & Costello, Dean Martin & Jerry Lewis, Laurel & Hardy, Chico Marx and Morey Amsterdam.

Home grown talent also appeared: Morecambe and Wise, Mike & Bernie Winters, Des O'Connor, Billy Dainty, Betty Driver, Jimmy Young, Marty Wilde, Max Bygraves, Harry Secombe, Cliff Richard and Billy Fury, and great support acts who helped to make the Empire the great variety theatre it was: Wilson, Keppel & Betty; Jimmy James & Co.; Stan Stennett; The Cox Twins; Dick Henderson; Walter Jackson, Clarkson & Leslie; Saveen & Daisy May; Cardini; Robert Earl; Chan Canasta; Hal Monty and all the others, too numerous to mention, but not forgotten.

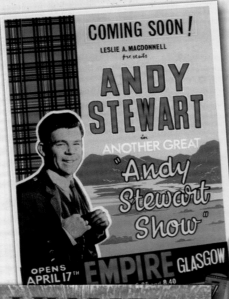

COMING SOON!

LESLIE A. MACDONNELL presents

ANDY STEWART

in ANOTHER GREAT

"Andy Stewart Show"

OPENS APRIL 17th   **EMPIRE** GLASGOW
6.25 and 8.40

King's Theatre BATH ST GLASGOW

CITY OF GLASGOW DISTRICT COUNCIL – Halls Department

Tuesday September 28th for TWO WEEKS ONLY

MONDAY – FRIDAY · 7.30 p.m.   SATURDAY – 5 p.m. & 8 p.m. 7/6

GLASGOW DISTRICT COUNCIL PRESENTS

GRACIE **CLARK & MURRAY** COLIN

'MR. & MRS. GLASGOW'

in 'The Best of CLARK & MURRAY'

A GOLDEN JUBILEE SHOW TO CELEBRATE
50 YEARS IN SHOWBUSINESS
WITH SPECIAL GUESTS

SALLY and JOE GORDON
LOU GRANT (1st Week Only) · RON DALE (2nd Week Only)
Alf Freeman : Ann Fields
Billy Little : Ginty McEwan
The May Moxon

MOSS' **Empire** THEATRE GLASGOW

Chairman: PRINCE LITTLER

6.25 ★ **MONDAY, NOV. 26th** ★ 8.40

TOP BRITISH VOICE OF THE TOP TEN

HIT RECORDS
OF
"MORE"
"THE MAN FROM LARAMIE"
"SOMEONE ON YOUR MIND"
"CHAIN GANG"

JIMMY YOUNG

THE VOICE OF DECCA RECORDS

WILSON KEPPEL   REID TWINS   RITA MARTELL   RONNIE COLLIS

PETER CRAWFORD   DONALD B. STUART   JOYCE GOLDING

ALHAMBRA

STEWART CRUIKSHANK presents

6d
PLEASE SEE
THAT THIS SEAL IS
UNBROKEN

Howard and Wyndham's

FIVE-PAST EIGHT

PROGRAMME

PERSONAL APPEARANCE

Prior to His Third Tour of Canada and America,
of
SCOTLAND'S GREAT COMEDIAN

ALEC FINLAY

in His Famous Character Studies.

GAIETY
6.30 THEATRE — AYR **8.40**

MONDAY, 20th APRIL   FOR 3 WEEKS

HALLMARK OF SENSATIONAL ENTERTAINMENT!!

PRIOR TO HIS GLASGOW PAVILION SEASON

THE
**LEX McLEAN
SUPER '70 SHOW**

WITH A STUPENDOUS ARRAY OF TALENT

Produced by BILLY DUNLOP

SCOTLAND'S KING OF COMEDY

CHARLIE   **MARGO**   **JIMMY**

JIM CASSIDY   ★   **BILLY HYGHGATE**

BOOK EARLY   **KEVIN ROSS**   **BOOK NOW**

HELEN RANDELL   ★   **THE MOXON LADIES**

BOX OFFICE
OPEN
10 a.m.—9 p.m.

...ok, or
...ne
...64639

... Oxford Street, Glasgow, C.5

EMPIRE GLASGOW Opening DEC. 11th for the Christmas Season   Douglas 6434 5.6

LESLIE A. MACDONNELL introduces

SIX GREAT SCOTTISH STARS
in
HAROLD FIELDING'S
£50,000 PANTOMIME SPECTACLE

CINDERELLA

with the Glorious Melodies of
RODGERS & HAMMERSTEIN

CALUM KENNEDY as the Prince   JOHNNY BEATTIE as Buttons   UNA McLEAN

MOSS' Empire

THEATRE GLASGOW

Proprietors: MOSS' EMPIRES, LTD.
Chairman: PRINCE LITTLER
Managing Director: VAL PARNELL
Telephone: DOUGLAS 6434/5/6
Manager: FRANK MATHIE

6.10 ★ **MONDAY, MARCH 28th**
TWICE NIGHTLY ★ **8.25**

AMERICA'S FABULOUS SINGING STARS
OF BRUNSWICK RECORDS

FIRST TIME IN BRITAIN

THE FOUR ACES

THE CRAZY FUNSTER
JOHNNY LOCKWOOD
RADIO AND TV'S STAR COMEDIAN

THE NICOLETTES DANCE TEAM	**RAF & JULIAN** LAUGHTER RAISERS	**THE YOLANDOS** Comedy with a Difference

MARGO *Essence of Versatility* **& SAM** **HENDERSON KEMP**

DASH'S CHIMPANZEES ALMOST HUMAN

TRIBE BROS., Ltd., London & St. Albans.

The Sunday Post - 6th July 2003

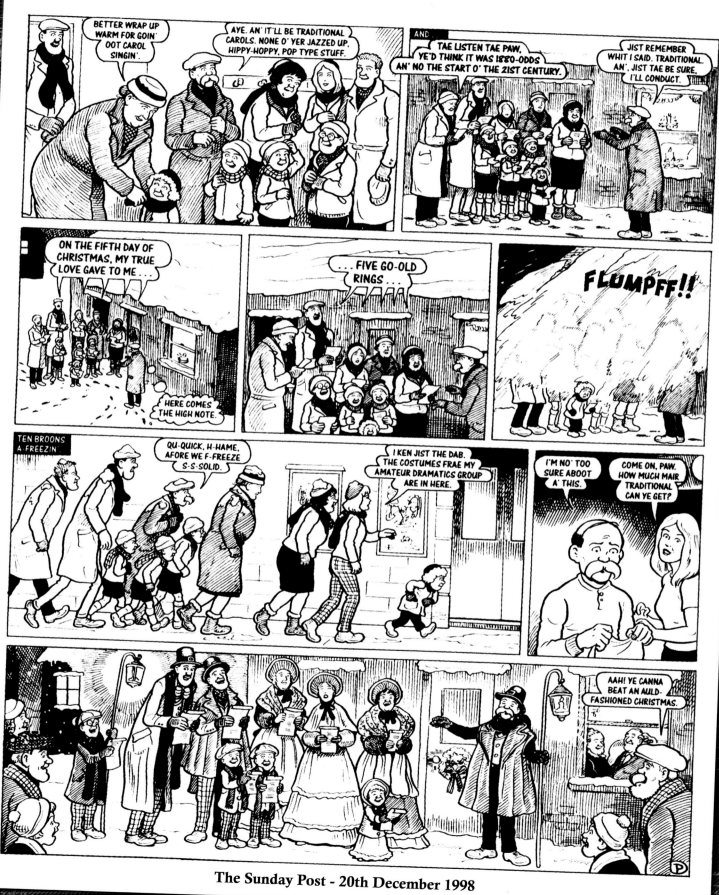

The Sunday Post - 20th December 1998

The Sunday Post - 27th December 1998

Will a' this exhausting work scupper —
—Maw and Paw's big Burns Supper?

The Sunday Post - 19th March 2000

The family all long—
—tae burst intae song!

The Sunday Post - 18th February 2001

Hen refuses to yield—
—aboot his antique shield!

The Sunday Post - 19th November 2000

The Sunday Post - 9th November 2003

Even Paw stops moaning—
The TV comes tae Number 10.

The Sunday Post - 28th December 2003

Hen thinks he kens the next big thing—
A brush, a comb an' a bit o' string.

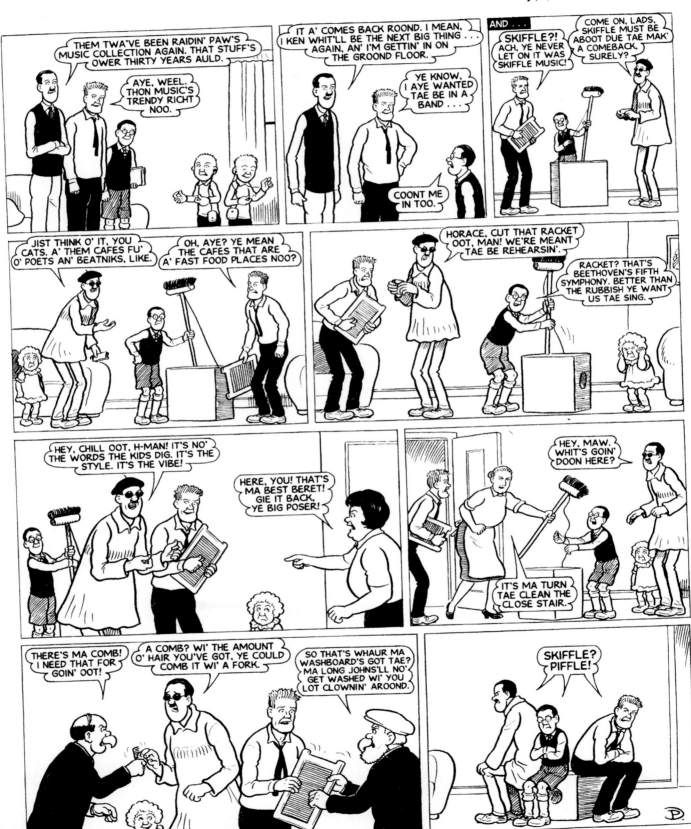

The Sunday Post - 8th December 2002

The Sunday Post - 21st August 2005

*Singin' isnae Granpaw's style—
but he can always raise a smile.*

The Sunday Post - 8th February 2004

Paw, the auld moan—
should've left things alone.

The Sunday Post - 11th April 2004

THE BAGPIPES

THE BAGPIPE is a musical wind-instrument of very great antiquity, having been used among the ancient Greeks and having been a favourite instrument in Europe since the fifteenth century.

It still continues in use among the country people of Poland, Italy, Brittany and the south of France, and in Scotland and Ireland, now often regarded as the national instrument of Scotland, especially Celtic Scotland.

It consists of a bag made of leather, (sheepskin or cowhide) which receives the air from the mouth (through the blow pipe), or from bellows; and of pipes, into which the air is pressed from the bag by the performer's elbow.

In the common or Highland form, one pipe (called the chanter) plays the melody; of the three others (called drones) two are in unison with the lowest A of the chanter, and the third and longest an octave lower, the sound being produced by means of reeds. The chanter is played with two hands, and has eight holes, which the performer stops and opens at pleasure, to produce the different notes but the scale is imperfect and the tone harsh. The chanter reed is made of two blades of cane joined by a ring of copper which vibrate against each other when air is forced between them.

The Highland bagpipe is a powerful instrument, and calls for great exertion of the lungs in order that the air may be supplied in sufficient quantity. The unique sound of the bagpipes combines a strong melody with a background accompaniment.

From 1st August 1746 until 1782, wearing kilts or tartan was illegal in Scotland. The 'Dress Act' was also used to stop people playing bagpipes.

Getting to know the bagpipes

A Bush
B Ring Cap
C Bass Drone Top
D Ferrule
E Tuning Pin
F Projecting Mount
G Bass Drone Mid Point
H Bass Drone Bottom Point
K Bass Drone Stock
L Tenor Top
M Tenor Joint
N Tenor Stock
P Blow Pipe Mouthpiece
R Blow Pipe Stock
S Pipe Chanter Stock
T Pipe Chanter
U Pipe Chanter Sole
V Bag Cover

A Bass Drone
B
C
D
E
F
G
H
K
P Blow Pipe
R
L Tenor Drone
M Tenor Drone
N
S
T
U Chanter
V

N AN' GRAN'PAW WERE RICHT ENOUGH.
E PIPES ARE GRAND FOR DANCIN' TAE AT THE NEW YEAR!

GASP-HOOCH!

MOSS' EMPIRE GLASGOW Theatre

Douglas 6434/5/6

Proprietors:
MOSS' EMPIRES LTD.

Chairman:
PRINCE LITTLER, C.B.E.

Managing Director:
LESLIE A. MACDONNELL, O.B.E.

Manager:
FRANK MATHIE

MONDAY
NOVEMBER 19th
TWICE NIGHTLY
6-25 & 8-40

"TARTAN TONICS"

A VARIETY COCKTAIL

"MRS ELRICK'S WEE SON"....

GEORGE ELRICK

YOUR COMPERE FROM RADIO'S "HOUSEWIVES CHOICE"

JIMMY SHAND

JUNIOR
AND HIS
COUNTRY
DANCE
BAND

CHARLIE STEWART & BETTY EMERY

JOHN & SUMA LAMONTE

CLARKSON & LESLIE

REY OVERBURY & SUZETTE

THE ROYAL SCOTTISH COUNTRY DANCE SOCIETY
(MEMBERS OF THE GLASGOW BRANCH)

DAVID BERGLAS

TELEVISION'S MAN OF MAGIC

ELECTRIC (Modern) PRINTING CO. LTD., MANCHESTER 8.

LiVE

FREE admishun!

in Wullie's shed

AUCHENSHOOGLE

A musikal eevenin'

← Wullie's shed

7 o'clock 'till bed time

"BEAT IT"

STARRING **OOr Wullie** and the gang

WANTED! → bucket drummer

NOT WANTED — P.C. Murdoch singin'

THE SUNDAY POST FUN SECTION
OOR WULLIE

The Sunday Post - 14th December 1947

The Sunday Post - 12th June 1949

Trombone, oompah, bagpipes, too—
That's Wullie and his "Tuneful Two"!

The Sunday Post - 27th June 1954

Oor Wullie joins the Tradesmen's Band—
But not the way that he had planned.

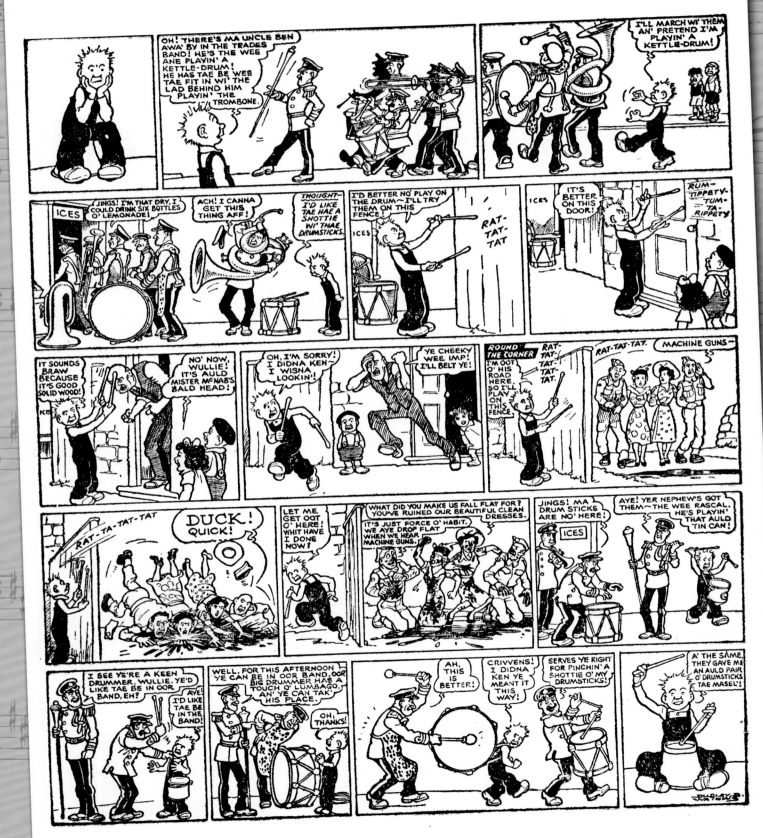

The Sunday Post - 3rd June 1951

The Sunday Post - 20th April 1952

The Sunday Post - 31st August 1952

He's in an orchestra today—
But not a note does Wullie play!

     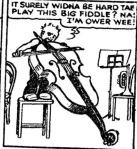

The Sunday Post - 10th April 1949

The Sunday Post - 24th February 1957

Wi' a hundred blaws an' a' and a'—
Oor Wullie scares the craws awa''!

The Sunday Post - 3rd October 1954

Most young musicians need a tutor—
But not Oor Wullie. He's much cuter!

ALHAMBRA THEATRE ★ GLASGOW

STEWART CRUIKSHANK presents

MAX BYGRAVES

in Fabulous 'FIVE PAST EIGHT' in the STARLIGHT ROOM

The BLUEBELL POLKA

METROPOLE THEATRE

Telephone: BELL 1734

WINTER SEASON

COMMENCING 9th DECEMBER. 1946
TWICE NIGHTLY
6·25 — 8·30

Alex. Frutin Presents

GORDON INGLIS'
GRAND XMAS & NEW YEAR ATTRACTION

OOR AIN FOLK
A GRAND SCOTTISH SPECTACLE

Written and Produced by GORDON INGLIS

SEE
The Big Novelty Surprise Finale

MATINEES Every Saturday at 2.15 p.m.

Xmas Week Wed., Thurs. & Sat.
Year Week

THE BIBLE TELLS ME SO

Words and Music by DALE EVANS

Recorded by THE PRINCE SISTERS on Decca Records

CHAPPELL & CO. LTD., 50 New Bond Street, London, W.I
PARAMOUNT—ROY ROGERS MUSIC CO. INC.
SOLE SELLING AGENT
FAMOUS MUSIC CORPORATION, 1619 BROADWAY NEW YORK 19, N.Y.

2/- NET

MADE IN ENGLAND

MOSS'

Empire

THEATRE GLASGOW

Proprietors: MOSS' EMPIRES LTD.   Telephone: DOUGLAS 6436/5'6
Chairman: PRINCE LITTLER   Managing Director: VAL PARNELL   Manager: FRANK MATHIE

6.25   OPENS TUES. DEC. 11th at 7.30   8.40   MATINEES at 2.30
       TWICE NIGHTLY   DECEMBER 15, 22, 25, 26, 29
                                              JAN. 1, 2, 5, 12, 19, 26 FEB. 2

TOM ARNOLD'S BIG NEW COMEDY SPECTACLE

WE'RE JOKING

A SUMPTUOUS NEW PRODUCTION with the PICK of SCOTLAND'S GREATEST ENTERTAINERS

CHIC MURRAY & MAIDIE

DUNCAN MACRAE
SCOTLAND'S GREAT PORTRAYER OF CHARACTERS

JACK ANTHONY
JACK'S THE BOY

ROBERT WILSON
THE VOICE OF SCOTLAND

DICK AND DOT REMY

ALEX DON

CLARKSON & LESLIE

WILL STARR

BERTH RICAR

and the BEAUX

STAGED BY CH

Prices of Admission
Stalls 4'-, 5'6, 6'6   Circle

Stalls 3'-, 4'6, 5'6
Circle 3'-, 4'-, 5'-

ALHAMBRA

STEWART CRUIKSHANK presents

XII XI X IX

6d.
PLEASE SEE THAT THIS SEAL IS UNBROKEN

Howard and Wyndham's

FIVE-PAST EIGHT

PROGRAMME

In dear old Glasgow Toon
(Hearts of Glasgow)

WORDS BY JOHN F. STEVENSON
MUSIC BY BILLY GRAHAM

Sung by Greci

GAIETY
THEATRE - AYR

Proprietors: KYLE AND CARRICK DISTRICT COUNCIL

Manager: BERNARD COTTON

Commencing Monday 9th May at 7.30 p.m.
Then for a Four Week Season
6.25 Twice Nightly 8.40

Scotland's Ambassador of Fun

RON DALE

in

"SCOTTISH SHOWTIME"

With MUSIC! SONG! and especially LAUGHTER! for all the family

Featuring TV and Recording Stars

JUNIPER GREEN

and

ROBERT JOHNSTONE • JOHN SHEARER
BETTY BRIGHT • WALTER PERRIE • KYLE DANCERS

and Special Guest —

WALTER CARR

From "The Vital Spark" and "Bonny"

Choreography by MARY PAYLING	Produced by DANNY REGAN	Musical Directors ALEX CAIRNS / WILL FYFFE Jr

Seat Prices £1.25, £1, 50p, with Reduced Rates for Children & Pensioners (exc. Saturdays)

BOX OFFICE OPEN 10 a.m. to 9 p.m.   Telephone Ayr (0292) 64639

T. M. Gemmell & Son Ltd., 100 High Street, Ayr

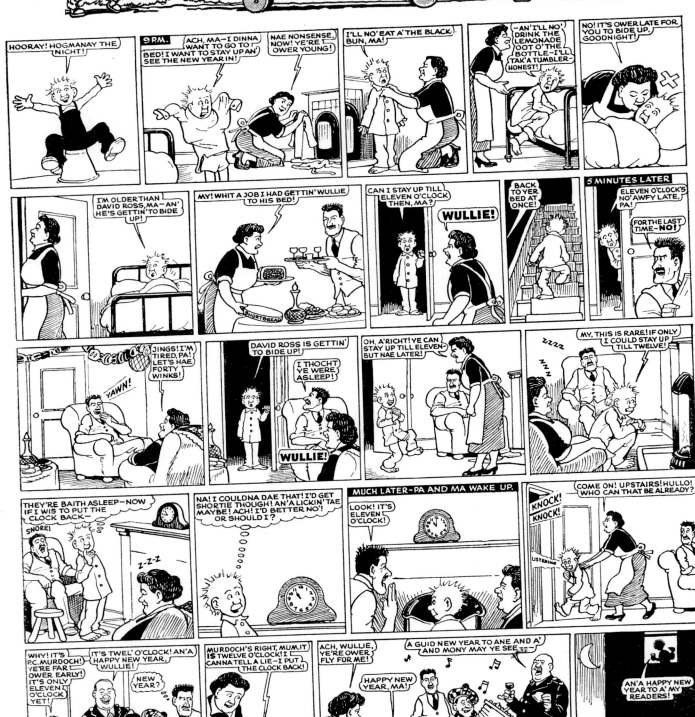

The Sunday Post - 28th December 1958

Oor Wullie's blawin' brings nae cheer,
But he gets a note—ye canna hear!

The Sunday Post - 16th August 1959

It's NOT the music, truth to tell.
That has wee Jeemy under a spell!

The Sunday Post - 6th October 1963

The Sunday Post - 15th May 1966

THE SUNDAY POST
FUN SECTION
OOR WULLIE

The Sunday Post - 24th March 1963

Oor Wullie marches doon the street—
He thinks his one-man band's a treat!

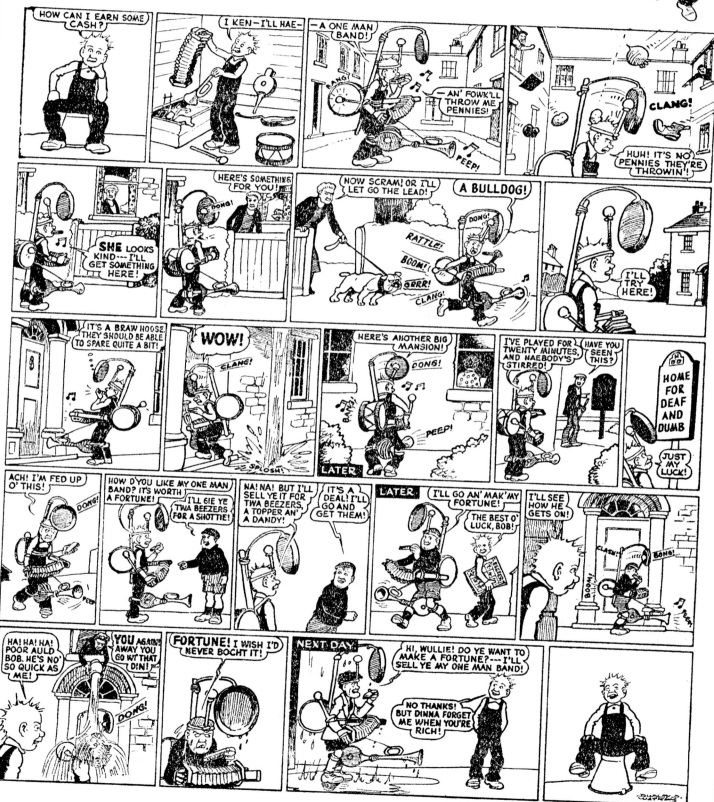

The Sunday Post - 16th September 1956

At the end o' the day, Wull "leads" the band—
But no' exactly as he planned!

OOR WULLIE

HE'S AWA' TAE A CONCERT WI' HIS UNCLE JIM.

IS THIS WHAUR WE HEAR SOME FUNNY ORCHESTRA, UNCLE JIM?

NO' SOME FUNNY ORCHESTRA'—A SYMPHONY ORCHESTRA.

THEY'RE PLAYIN' BEETHOVEN'S UNFINISHED SYMPHONY IN C MINOR, WULLIE.

HA-HA! THAT MUST BE 'C' FOR COAL—COAL 'MINOR'!

THIS IS BRAW!

THAT WIS GREAT, UNCLE JIM! I THINK I'LL START MY AIN ORCHESTRA.

NEXT DAY—

RIGHT, LADS, WE'LL START OFF WI' A SELECTION O' CHICKOVSKY'S LATEST HITS.

WAIL!

SCREECH! THUMP!

WHIT'S A' THIS DIN? YE'VE WOKEN MY BAIRN!

SORRY, MISSUS! RUN FOR IT, LADS!

LET'S GO DOON TAE TONI'S CHIPPER. I'VE GOT A GREAT IDEA.

A'RIGHT, WULLIE, I GIVE YOU A TRY.

YE'LL HAE A HIGH CLASS ORCHESTRA SERENADIN' YER CUSTOMERS.

HOWL!

WHAT'S THAT YOU SAY? I NO' HEAR YOU RIGHT.

TWA PUDDEN SUPPERS AN' A SINGLE FISH!

ACH, NEVER MIND! YE CANNA HEAR YERSEL THINK WI' THAT RACKET GOIN' ON!

BLARE!

SORRY, BOYS. ORCHESTRAS IS NO' GOOD FOR BUSINESS. YOU GO NOW, PLEASE.

ACH, OKAY, TONI.

I KEN! WE CAN PRACTISE IN THE AULD BANDSTAND IN THE PARK!

WOOYEEOOOEEEEE

THAT'S IT, BOAB! YE'RE FAIR GETTIN' THE HANG O' THON FIDDLE!

EXCUSE ME, LADS. I HEARD YE PLAYIN', AN' I WORK FOR THE COONCIL. I'D LIKE YE TAE PLAY AT THE BAIRD HALL THE NIGHT.

GREAT!

THIS IS OOR BIG CHANCE! WE COULD GO RIGHT TAE THE TOP!

STAGE

AYE, YE'LL CERTAINLY GO RIGHT TAE THE TOP!

JIST PLAY UP ON THE ROOF FOR AN HOUR OR SO TAE STOP A' THESE STARLINGS FROM ROOSTIN' HERE!

WE CAN AYE SAY WE HAD AN AUDIENCE O' THOOSANDS!

The Sunday Post - 3rd November 1985

A yacht becalmed? See Wullie's wheeze—
He quickly conjures up a breeze!

The Sunday Post - 27th June 1982

The Sunday Post - 18th August 1985

OOR WULLIE

The Sunday Post - 7th March 1988

A Personal Message
To All "Met" Patrons
From
JIMMY LOGAN

Metropole Theatre
Glasgow

TAE OOR AIN FOLK
WHEREVER THEY MAY BE!

In the Past we have Presented a Festive Show for Christmas and
New Year and I am pleased to say that we have hit the "Jackpot"
with an average attendance of 250,000 satisfied Customers during our
Winter Show.

This Year we will present the ...

THE METROPOLE THEATRE
PROUDLY WELCOMES
TO THE BIG SHOW

Scotland's Great Comedian
The King of Laughter

BILLY RUSK

See Me! See Me!

★ ★ ★

THE FREEMEN
Stuart, Alf and Brian

SCOTLAND'S PREMIER VOCAL TRIO!

★ ★ ★

6.30   8.40

GAIETY
THEATRE, AYR

● TWO WEEKS ONLY — COMMENCING MONDAY, 21st OCTOBER ●

POPPLEWELLS PRESENT A PHENOMENAL ATTRACTION

TOAST to the TARTAN
Devised and Produced by ANTONY MAYNE

STARRING
THE GOLDEN VOICE OF THE HIGHLANDS

CALUM KENNEDY
on his first visit to Ayr

| SAMMY SHORTT | THE HEATHER ISLE TRIO | ANTONY MAYNE |
| WILL STARR | THE HEATHER ISLE ... | KEN SWAN |

See the Big Scenic Spectacle

ROTHESAY BAY BY MOONLIGHT
DUMARTE AND DENZER
PRESENTING 100 SKELETONS

THE FREEMEN
THE SONG GROUP PAR EXCELLENCE

THE TEN MOXON MAIDS
BRAEMAR LADIES PIPE BAND
50 - STAR ARTISTES - 50

Booking Form

To The Manager,
THE METROPOLE THEATRE, St. George's Cross, Glasgow, C.3.

Dear Sir,
Please book the following seats for my party:

STALLS.................................... 6.25 | 8.30 | Matinee   Date................

CIRCLE.................................... 6.25 | 8.30 | Matinee   Date................
            (Please delete performance not required)

Matinee every Saturday as from 3rd December at 2.15 p.m.
Holiday Matinees 2nd, 3rd, 4th & 7th January, 1967

PRICES OF ADMISSION:

Monday to Thursday, 1st House Friday and Saturday Matinees   ....   STALLS, 7/6   CIRCLE, 6/6
2nd House Fridays, Saturdays and Holidays   ....   STALLS, 8/6   CIRCLE, 7/6
All Performances 26th December — 7th January (Inclusive) at Holiday Prices

Name..

Address..

....

PLEASE BOOK EARLY—BOOKING OFFICE Telephone - DOUglas 9191-9192 (2 Lines)

PLEASE DETACH AND POST TO MANAGER

BOOK YOUR PARTY FOR

Jimmy Logan's
METROPOLE
Glasgow

1966 — WINTER SHOW — 1967

'THE SKIRL O' THE PIPES'

Produced by DANNY REGAN

Grand Opening Gala Performance
THURSDAY, 17th NOVEMBER at 7.30 p.m.

THEREAFTER AT 6.25 AND 8.30 p.m.
MATINEES SATURDAYS AT 2.15 p.m.

BOOK NOW!

50p

MOSS' Empire THEATRE GLASGOW

Proprietors: MOSS' EMPIRES LTD.
Chairman: PRINCE LITTLER
Managing Director: VAL PARNELL
Telephone: DOUGLAS 6434/5/6
Manager: FRANK MATHIE

6.25 ★ **MONDAY, MARCH 10th** ★ **8.40**
TWICE NIGHTLY

JACK ANTHONY
WITH
BERTHA RICARDO
BOND ROWELL

THE CLYDE VALLEY STOMPERS
WITH
MARY MacGOWAN

ANN AND VAL

ROBERT WILSON
AND THE
WHITE HEATHER GROUP
WITH
GORDON MacKENZIE
WILL STAR
DENIS WOOLFORD
& SYDNEY DEVINE

BILLY CROTCHET
WITH
DIZZY KRAZY KOMEDY

SHELLEY 'TAP OF THE BILL'
JIMMY FLETCHER

KEN & ALLAN HAYNES
WITH A PIANO

The Sunday Post - 5th February 1992

Wullie cannae get a cheep!
His bagpipes need the chimney sweep!

The Sunday Post - 26th November 1995

The reviews are certainly far fae glowin' . . .
. . . for Murdoch's voice an' Wullie's bowin'.

The Sunday Post - 8th June 1997

The Sunday Post - 22nd June 1997

The Sunday Post - 24th March 1996

Wullie thinks it's no sae braw . . .
. . . when he gies these pipes a blaw.

The Sunday Post - 24th August 1997

Here's a thing that wasnae planned—
  —Wull's been banned frae the pipe band!

The Sunday Post - 10th May 1998

The Sunday Post - 2nd August 2001

Wullie has tae dangle—
—the school band's triangle!

The Sunday Post - 16th May 1999

THE COMB

GROOMING UTENSIL OR UNUSUAL MUSICAL INSTRUMENT?

A musical instrument is quite simply anything used for the purpose of making sounds. Anything that makes a sound can be a musical instrument, but it is in its use to make music that the object becomes a musical instrument.

Such instruments can be traced back to early man. A drum was made from animal skin or a simple pipe perhaps – the blowing through a reed or hollow cane or instruments made from wood or bone was the early wind instrument.

Simple flutes were more sophisticated early instruments.

Early woman created the first combs and examples have been found by archaeologists at digs dating back more than 5,000 years.

The combs were wooden or bone toothed devices used for straightening, styling and cleaning hair.

The simple comb was one of the most important tools of civilization and is still in use today.

It seems logical that after the invention of the comb that its use as a musical instrument would follow, but it was itself not a useful drumstick so man invented the papermaking process, to allow it to evolve and be popularised as a musical instrument in its own right.

We know from 2nd century BC discoveries in China of early archaeological fragments of paper found close to combs of different lengths and materials that man has made music with comb and paper from that time on.

The urge to play a comb is a basic human instinct.

Just as man realised the potential,

a few simple guidelines like those passed from cave to cave and campfire to campfire are all you need to play like your ancestors – and you can master the comb and paper in a single day.

Any comb will do to begin, but you will soon learn to experience the effect which different lengths and thicknesses of comb can have on your musical style.

Some voice training may enhance the experience as it is the vibration and control of the voice which is at the heart of the art.

The choice of paper is crucial. It needs to be big enough to fold over the teeth of the comb, and the length

should be just shorter than the comb itself.

Greaseproof kitchen paper is perfect; newspaper works particularly well, but in the same

THE COMB-OVER

1 If, like Paw Broon, you have that flyaway type of hair, your FREE comb will serve doubly well as a grooming device.

HOW TO PLAY THE COMB

1 Lay the comb flat on top of the sheet of paper.

YOU'LL FIND YOUR FREE COMB AND PAPER INSIDE THE COVER OF THIS BOOK.

2 Fold the paper over the comb.

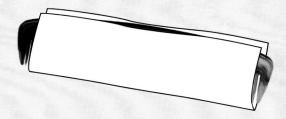

3 Your comb is prepared and ready to make beautiful music.

way as you should be wary of using coloured tissue qualities or cheap giftwrap, enthusiastic players may develop inky lips as the newsprint or tissue dye transfers to the lips.

When used in a concert these elements are, in the modern world, sometimes known as a comb kazoo.

To start, grip the comb, teeth down, flat in front of you.

Take the folded paper and place it as you would a tent over a ridgepole and hold the edges of the paper and the comb together.

Place the comb close to your lips which should be closed.

Now you are ready to play!

Start humming a tune but keep the comb quite still in front of you. The vibration from your voice which you can feel in your teeth will cause the paper to vibrate against the teeth of the comb.

The pitch of your voice dictates the sounds which are transmitted to the comb.

If you can hum you can make a comb kazoo sing!

If you become proficient and gather a portfolio of tunes and develop the essential head-nodding and body-swaying techniques which enhance the whole experience, you can be the envy of your friends and neighbours as an entertainer and musician.

With imagination, there are no limits to what you can achieve.

2 Utilise your comb to gather precious hair strands.

3 Neatly fold strands over the top of the head. A quick glance in a mirror is advisable to check for any odd hair positioning.

4 Voilà! A perfectly acceptable hairstyle to be proud of with which to venture out into the world.

Tae hear this lot bicker an' bellow—
Ye wouldnae think jazz wis meant tae be mellow!

The Sunday Post - 23rd July 2000

HE'S AWA' OOT WI' FAT BOB.

 LISTEN – I CAN HEAR BAGPIPES. ME, TAE.

 WHIT RARE – THE POLIS PIPE BAND ARE HAEIN' A PRACTICE.

 SWING IT, BOB. GAUN YERSEL', WULLIE.

 HERE – I KEN THE MANNIE ON THE BIG DRUM. IT'S P.C. MURDOCH.

 TEN MINUTE BREAK, LADS.

 JINGS! IT MUST BE BRAW TAE PLAY THE BIG DRUM.

 AYE, IT IS – WID YE LIKE A WEE SHOTTIE? WID I NO' JUST?

 MICHTY! IT'S HEAVIER THAN I THOCHT!

 UP YE GET, WULLIE. TA, BOB.

 HELP! NO' SAE FAR UP, YE PUDDEN! OOPS!

 DINNAE DAMAGE MY GUID DRUM. WH-WHIT ABOOT M-M-ME?

 AT LEAST HE'S STOPPED. HELP!

 IT'S A' RICHT. I REPEAT – WHIT ABOOT ME?

 JINGS! MY HEID'S BIRLIN' NOO.

 ACH, NEVER MIND, WULLIE – IT'S NO' A'BODY THAT CAN DAE A DRUM ROLL.

 YON DRUM HAD THE BEATIN' O' ME!

The Sunday Post - 14th April 2002

The Sunday Post - 19th June 2005

Wouldn't it be fine and grand—
Bein' a drummer in a band?

Wull had fun on his own—
Wi' a big trombone!

The Sunday Post - 20th August 2006

Wullie's heavy rockin' is somethin' truly shockin'!

The Sunday Post - 18th March 2004

EDINBURGH TATTOO

In the past, as today, the duties of military drummers require them to make routine calls during the day to day life of the Regiment, both in the field and in barracks, either as individuals or as a Corps of Drums. Two of these routine calls were the Tattoo and the Retreat.

It is thought that the expression 'Tattoo' is derived from the Dutch Doe Den Tap Toe, 'Turn off the taps', and dates from the time when the British Army was fighting in the Low Countries.

In the 18th century it was the custom for armies to go in to winter quarters until a spring offensive could be launched. It was the practice for the soldiers to be billeted in the towns and villages and naturally the social life of these men revolved around the town. The innkeepers turned off their beer taps at ten o'clock to indicate to the soldier that he had to return to his billet; this was notified to the innkeeper and the soldiers by a drummers' Tattoo. An officer, sergeant and drummer would commence the beating and after a set time they would set off through the towns, with the drummer beating his call, and as they moved through the town the officer and sergeant would ensure that all the men had left by checking each ale house in turn.

As time went on this practice of calling the troops to quarters was enriched occasionally by adding fifers and playing tunes (in Scottish regiments pipers replaced fifers). This made a more cheerful sound than the lone drum. A final addition to this custom was the Band and hence the Tattoo became a display of drums and music by torchlight to entertain the Garrison and led finally to the idea of a 'Tattoo' as a military pageant.

THE ROYAL EDINBURGH MILITARY TATTOO

The most famous of these is The Royal Edinburgh Military Tattoo – performed by British Armed Forces, British Commonwealth and International military bands and display teams.

The Tattoo is performed on Edinburgh Castle's esplanade, in August of each year.

■ Edinburgh Castle. Home to the Royal Edinburgh Military Tattoo.

Tattoo Facts

■ The first Edinburgh Tattoo took place in 1950. There were eight items in the programme. Since then more than 12 million people have attended the Tattoo. The annual audience is over 200,000. In addition, more than 100 million people see the Tattoo each year on international television.

■ The first commercial twelve-inch stereo LP record of the Tattoo was released in 1961.

■ The first overseas regiment to participate was the Band of the Royal Netherlands Grenadiers. The year was 1952, and there were also performers from Canada and France.

■ The first lone piper was Pipe Major George Stoddart. He played in every performance for the first eleven years. His son, Major Gavin Stoddart, followed his father as lone piper at the Tattoo and became Director of Army Bagpipe Music for 12 years.

■ The Tattoo has always been staged at Edinburgh Castle. Rehearsals take place at Redford Barracks in Edinburgh.

Over 40 countries have been represented at the Tattoo.

■ There are usually five or six pipe bands massed in the Edinburgh Tattoo. The infantry battalions of the Scottish Division are always well represented and the regular services will provide at least one other band – perhaps from the Guards, the Cavalry, the Gurkhas or the Royal Air Force. The musicians in these bands are all fighting servicemen for whom combat must take priority over piping and drumming. In the infantry, for example, the pipe band usually has the official role of battalion machine gun platoon.

THE EDINBURGH MILITARY TATTOO 1963

A.E. HASWELL MILLER

THE EDINBURGH FESTIVAL

PROGRAMME 1/-

■ Vintage programme from the 1963 Tattoo.

OOR WULLIE

OOR WULLIE

P.C. Murdoch
MUSIC CORRESPONDENT

GOLDEN BUGLES AWARDED DESPITE CO-OPERATIVE HA' FARCE

I'm just back fae the Co-operative Ha' where Tam McDougall was the host for The Auchentogle's Got Talent Music Competition.

Due tae a mix-up wi' the bookin' arrangements with the ha', the competition wis double booked wi' the Glebe Street Care Home for the Perplexed & Bewildered's Tea Dance.

So it turned oot that there wis music an' occasional dancin', and mair pressure on the conveniences.

The plan was that the secret and anonymous judges were scattered round the ha' tae avoid the chance o' jiggery pokery, and them bein' plied wi drink fer their favours, like the last competition which ended up in a shambles.

But this time,when it came time for the judgin' Tam had tae ca' a'body tae attention wi' the microphone. As he announced: "It seems that the secret and anonymous judging panel that wis scattered round the ha' have indeed been compromised wi' mair jiggery pokery, efter a' and fower o' them fell asleep, anither twa are no' tae be found onywhere, so we've nae option but tae be declarin' the contest null and void. Jock McHill will be returnin' a' the bets – so if ye make an orderly queue ye'll get yer money back."

Poor Tam wis booed aff the stage for the second year runnin'.

But a'body had performed their hearts oot so, in my capacity as The Auchentogle Bugle's Music Correspondent, I'm going to award Golden Bugles for whit I thocht were outstanding turns.

OUTSTANDING FEMALE SOLO ACT – DAPHNE BROON

BEST GROUP OR ENSEMBLE – THE BROONS FAMILY

EMERGING ARTISTS AWARD – OOR WULLIE & HIS BUCKET DRUMMERS

BEST SOLO MUSICIAN – GRANPAW BROON ON THE ACCORDION

Here's the report fae the night itsel':
It a' got goin' wi' a wee bit ceilidh music – some o' the guests fae the Glebe Street home were tappin' their feet afore we'd even stairted – that's how excited they were as they welcomed Albert McFarlane & His

BEST SOLO

Daphne Broon.

Ceilidh Band.

Then it wis the Broons Bairn and The Twins singin' *Coulter's Candy*, which wis rare – they got a great big clap.

"NE'ER BE WI'OOT A BUGLE - YER NEWS, YER VIEWS "

Magical night of song and dance

The Broons – should be in a class of their own!

There wis a duet o' one man bands – Oor Wullie an' Granpaw Broon, and Granpaw stayed on the stage as the Co-operative Ha's answer tae Jimmy Shand, The Wizard o' the box, and he gave a fine, spirited rendition that reminded me o' a wee story. How can you tell if there's an accordion player at the door? He doesn't know if he is to come in and he cannae find the key onyway!

And The Broons Family took the stage – whit a musically talented family they are tae! They certainly should be in a class by themselves.

And then the wild card of the night sponsored by *The Sunday Post* – It wis *The Fun Section* playing a wee bit country and western.

I always feel sorry for the piano player – having to work with instrumentalists who just cannae keep up. I love it. Another wee joke – What happens when you play country western music backwards?

You get your pickup truck back, your dog comes back tae life, and you get back your job at the car wash.

Next, a' the way fae Auchenshoogle – Oor Wullie's favourite – The Boogalusa Cajun Band. They had a request for *The Yellow Rose of Texas*. They didnae play that exact tune, but it' had a lot of the same notes in it.

The stars o the ivories gave us a musical treat – Joe, Horace an' Hen Broon played *The Glebe Street Medley* arranged by Horace – o' *Chopsticks*, *The Blue Danube* and *Danny Boy* – fae the classic collection *Duets For Six Hands*.

It brought tears to my eyes.

BUCKETS TAE CHEER ABOOT

ELDEST PERFORMER

BEST EMERGING ARTISTS

Best emerging artists – Oor Wullie and his bucket drummers.

Granpaw Broon wis asked tae play 'Far Far Away'.

My ain contribution tae the evenin' was what I thocht wis a grand rendition o' *O Sole Mio*. It's no' for me tae sing my ain praises but if ye'd like tae write in tae the readers' letters page, I'll hae a look.

And, after me, marchin' in the back door o' the ha' inspired by the Royal Edinburgh Military Tattoo – it wis Oor Wullie an' his marchin' bucket drummers. They were a great turn.

Wullie wis saying efter that he gave Fat Bob two sticks so he could become a drummer, but he lost one and became a conductor instead.

And then a'thing wis calmed doon as the lovely Broons Sisters Daphne and Maggie took their turns – Daphne singin' *Ae Fond Kiss* and Maggie – *My Love Is Like a Red Red Rose*.

We were a' greetin'!

At the final interval we were entertained by our Tea Dance guests fae the Glebe Street Carehome. We a' took the floor for *The Politician's Dance* – guided by Tam "All you have to do is take three steps forward, two steps backward, then side-step side-step, and turn around."

There wis a vote o' thanks tae Maw Broon an' her efternoon tea ladies for layin' on a magnificent spread: the sausage rolls and sandwiches and all the hospitality. She said – "It's a' aboot makin' your guests feel like they're at home, even if you wish they were."

We're a' gonnae try again next year – get yer washboards oot!